Walk the Wildly

Also by Lizz Murphy

Shebird (PressPress 2016)
Portraits: 54 Poems (PressPress 2013)
Six Hundred Dollars (PressPress 2010)
Stop Your Cryin (Island Press 2004)
Two Lips Went Shopping (Spinifex Press 2000)
Pearls and Bullets (Island Press 1997)
*Do Fish Get Seasick (*Polonius Press 1994)

Lizz Murphy
Walk the Wildly

PICARO PRESS

Acknowledgements

'Absence' was previously published in *Blue Dog: Australian Poetry* Volume 7 #14 and 'Landslips' in *Going Down Swinging* Issue 28. 'If Words were Fish' was published in the exhibition catalogue *Conversations: Five Artists, Five Writers*, Goulburn Regional Art Gallery. 'If Words were Fish', 'Memory' and 'Red to Black' were written as part of *Conversations*. 'Difficult to be Here' was written for *Prose Sculpture 2: Writing within Writing*, 31st Franco-Anglais Poetry Festival 2008. 'Place' and 'What Angel' were shared on Poneme with thanks. Even more thanks go to Thursday's with Yeats for fruitful frivolities over cake and creations.

Walk the Wildly
ISBN 978 1 920957 86 5
Copyright © text Lizz Murphy 2009

This edition published 2017 by
Picaro Press – an imprint of
GINNINDERRA PRESS
PO Box 3461 Port Adelaide 5015 Australia
www.ginninderrapress.com.au

Contents

Walk the Wildly	7
Fox	12
Hitched	14
Blackbird	15
Magpie	18
Out of the Side of My Eye	19
Out of the White	20
How Will I Describe	21
Place	22
Country	23
Landslips	24
Introduction to a Poem	25
Salt	26
Absence	27
If Words Were Fish	28
Never Turn Your Back	29
Memory	30
Difficult to Be Here	31
What Angel	32
Red to Black	33
Taxi	34

Walk the Wildly

Walk the wildly wending hoof-path Sloping slanting
unreconciled land Oak sideboards cast iron keys
cutlery drawers clover-lined Pasture grazed down to
green felt Taunting rain The rise around the dam a grin
or a way-finding song Are you sure you don't journey
alone when you sing? I saw her mouth I saw her eyes
how quickly she incubated that decision
Her full peaty throttle

It's a lumbering lantern-jawed season
It rubs its hands together
sidles you into its chilly core
and all that might not be determined

☙

>On the heel of visible breath
>nightfall is an unheard voice
>or an unabashed robe

>Strike the first fire
>Flame settling unleashing harlequin birds
>hear them divide seed beetle bark
>Flame murmuring
>Your warm ear funnelling
>another relentless drumming

>Underglow

>Bodies like mulled wine

Animal sounds big enough to break open the door
The hearth and its small sighs hugs of warmth

☙

The picnics of their youth
Sidewinding snaking on elbows shoulder blades
heels working their way under house-size granite
Above their bold faces a cool stone gallery

She imagines the art created this way
how many millennia before
cradles a coolamon of awe
through her decades
Any upheaval of the earth unfathomed
the hacking contraction
faulting shifting the tightening of its belt
seismic thrusts tilts the quarrel of the grain

Now it is private ground
our hands stained ochre
chains stencilled on their backs
No trespassers tolerated

☙

    Whirring foraging looping cirrus
    wool roving agitated into a shawl
    fit for the gods

    Handsome dog head
    in flat-top window
    Panting

☙

	Old man
Revving	dark drape
Petrol	
Exhaust	The shipwreck of his back
	one foot rowing air
	ankles with the skin of Brown Turkey Figs

                Smoke in hand
                burn in chair
                shifting
                creaking
                The adroit revision of tales
                scuttering like crabs from his stock

                His camp bed
                his sleep-out
                did he ever have a wife

Steak and kidney pies in bakery bags
Friendly strangers Baseball cap greetings
You can see some of them are jesters
Chests enlisted for a cause
read my T-shirt

                    ☙

She pleats her story into the brevity of our
purchase The store dances like sherbet
Floorboards adjust The quick step of her slender
feet the footprint of generations intact history
long talk early mornings Her father their shop
foxtrot music waltz spin a Gay Gordon
community glue We believe every word she will

have photographs and other trophies she is the
type My mother my life emerges from a rear
doorway her ankles are cream mixing bowls the
rattlesnake shake of wooden spoons the pigeon-
wing whisk rub butter into flour frost finger tips
separate the egg weigh measure They are
women of precise skirts folds ironed into flint
hemmed decency nicking their shins

> A single cabinet elegant self-assured glassy-eyed
> brassy sighly floats in the Oregon expanse
> the toothy cheddar the ham off the bone

❧

Passions pucker transform worlds
curate the senses
A lit room

> Stoics folded like clean clothing or thin smiles
> The tidal lock of the bloodthirsty moon
> The invention of the clock the girdle of time
> you are late you are early you are sprung
> you are wound up The garment of suspicion
> the bottom of the basket the domestic thrum
> and knock of assumption

> Words sharking
> from the big sea-run
> of their mouths
> the ditch overboard
> the nautical miles
> permission to dock

                                      His one eye is a hammer blow
                          He can't remember where he lost the other

                                               ❧

The greening calm of recovering ground

                                               ❧

Bereaved white plains still ahead
questioning sun
motherless hills biting at the lower sky
the unfurling stain of no tenure

Outside the edge of leaves
the edge of deliberation
capricious memory

                                             There they are left
                                  standing by their convictions
                                            parallel travellers
                                            watching over luggage

Fox

That fresh-faced fox-morning
Farmers' sheds legging it over hills
smocked with tractor tracks plough lines
ribbing rubbing fencelines

Hill dweller black-brown fur-shredded bone-red roadkill
A glove dust-blackened spins in the wake fingers separating air
Destiny scratches turf stiff-limbed long-nailed your words
swallowed in its silent stretched throat Time is a silver fish

When fish swim by you know it's rained enough
The endless drive home of someone without one
white lines splashing off into clouds grey as grief
All that ammunition spent on road signs and the dead
cold as four skun rabbits he said were frozen in one block

The storm is a fast shadow
a thousand nights shot through
a symphony of sordid screams
Look out fox-friend
keep your skin
wash your hide in the last drop
The country so thin
a hard knuckle of a woman

Spine-sawing twisting trickery
Her rough foxy passage
Wire netting ironbark hemp rope
A mosaic of delft glass
and more chimeless bones

Dream summer shake light
An ember burning through the sky
Eternity is a whisper beneath a forest of leaves
What part of the mouth is your emotion in
frantic friend leave your vision there on watch
by the smooth repulsive chain

A couple turn in a doorway
Their breezy ribbon arms
loosely woven around the heat
They pick toeholds in amber resistance
For all their protests what do they stop

In the distance a call of fire

        Fire!
        Fire!

    That red fox

Hitched

The sky is a collapse of stones the air an animal
It's dim breath a wish on the throat Spring is a
baking back early blossoms fig buds by the house
local birds unfriendly that nest-building tradition
hurling fear into their eyes afternoon walks
curtailed by abrupt ducks and dives

Untimely frost is a trollop it wipes out everything
that is tender Every year they are surprised by this
as if without rain for so long all the other elements
should shrivel fold into themselves Their dreams
are perverse ice-rich adventures quake lakes
ancestral places Stars spray this universe like ash
or sweat collected on their hammering flanks

They inspect the brash blue daily their foreheads
strained like fence wire but there they are again
toasting sandwiches for lunch barking their
elbows on their hitched up rough it out lives

Blackbird

Bushlark hands
empty swirl and rinse
fresh-baked terracotta

I hear the slide of leaves
as olive residue separates
reveals fine scarlet threads

Here I am with a worriment
I tell anyone listening in
the hills collapsing into themselves

The adult rosellas have parasites
They are snips of red cotton
the sweepings after dressmaking

The unsewn moments
of this warm
loose-mouthed afternoon

Earlier we heard the blackbird
playing flutes from the spire
of its conifer cathedral

That melodic intruder
its precise tangerine beak
scissoring at the sky

And the raiding currawongs
with their priestly wings
and hook-beak frenzy

Sweetmeat hatchlings
the tear of earth
the choir of keening magpies

Then the silent flyover
Younger red-green natives
captured only in the surprise
of transitory shapes

Swift tattoos across sparse lawn
the grey grill of grevillea
the ridged roof robust in all seasons
its iron whisperings coaxing in a cold front

How long till the blackbird is back
foraging finding invertebrates
in undergrowth shrinking into itself

How long before a fledgling
its feathers the stain of tended soil
runs an unsteady length of broken board

Or a juvenile flying the shortest of spans
flagging gutter to slumping branch
And game again on the veranda
launches itself in a gay splatter

Its stiff limbs like poking fingers
its panting spotted breast
pressing a path through space

First empty nest then empty distance
You recognise the wind of chance
in their jubilant eyes

They are full of the new life
have found their own uncompassed way
Just like you told them they would
Like you told them they should

It has caught my generation short
the skin of it settling over the migratory pass
Streamflows knotting around long unmoving stones
shucking their occupant souls together

They have the vacant knock of brass
The bell strike of hammer on nail
The scuff of spade entering sod
The rasp of the smallest of the deaths

Magpie

Fretting for song
he chants question marks
Steals meat
Absconds
A rackety
shook out overcoat

Out of the Side of My Eye

Black umbrella
open fold open
A raven navigates
lean timbers
loping woods

Out of the White

I wrap in bramble red
under white of afternoon
its cockatoo blades
its ratchety talk
raking up the hills

Out of the white
Out of the racketing chill
Its flight path my sigh
as I prepare for that tercel
the unrested city

Its unflinching neck
a lunette a cranking handle
Two mustard feet
turnkeys in a toy tin plane

One ringed eye
on the grimalkin by the gate
One fixed on the dam
a reducing circumference
Wafermarks

This place so often too far
so often too small
so often just big enough
so often
so softening

How Will I Describe

The eyes are language in damaged flight
the underwing glaze of an old-fashioned vase
kicked snow or the skin on boiled milk
heavily salted olives (green)
crestfallen windows or naked birds
blue as harmony earth shaken clean

Place

You must be in a strong place
Are you in a strong place?

There are sleek iron bars
on all sides
and in me
carved cedar

Is there right of entry?

Rostered light whiskers
Frost crystallises

And at night is the cat face?

The cat is inverted
not able to look itself in the lion swipe
A thorn of red beak
The white eye

There was a thorn once
Was it removed?

As I am

Country

With thanks to Lisel Mueller

I acknowledge not the ocean but the river
The sea put aside for special occasions
You paddle a long way to find depth
The river is for the everyday
I walk its wide and green observe under-bridge creatures
One grandfather is a cameo of wisdom
The grandmother a rosebud brooch
My father's parents survive longer I am their catch
My country is in pieces much goes unsaid our mouths squandered
We sail to the large continent where you needn't take umbrellas
The language slow from heat and unfinished endings
I feel foreign in it
In my country it rains blue aerograms
Adolescence is another dangerous place
I like to be outside
I meet you before the landslide
We make ordinary lives not so ordinary
My mother is a wren
That past drifts close again
My father still gifts me earth embedded words
I see my children are more grown than I am
I am in that otherworld before and aft country

Landslips

Look down that squinty street
where the greasy moon hovers
floodlights the turret chimney-run

Your rawboned hand
roams to that white place
your fingers are linnets
leave strange wings

Haphazard seas drown us out
grainy winds row us in
no words for the landslips
the whitebait of our memories

We didn't take enough photos
We said that

Introduction to a Poem

after Billy Collins

A poem
is a black cat walking luck into your journey
See how it twists its spine to land you
on all four legs
What a fine parachute it makes

Take its silk
and fashion a child a frock
a tent for the homeless
a curtain for a poet's cell

Or spin a deep river
Remember your life jacket
You don't have to understand water
to drown in it

Salt

i.
She scrutinises the salty shoreline
squeezes deception on to glass
Her cold sea palette

ii.
Her two hands the ocean rush
A greedy tide a kelp forest

iii.
She paints his violet-eye drowning
tastes his salt mouth adds relish

iv.
Casuarina curtain
Moody water
Salt-cool slippers her feet

Absence

Recount the three chokes of fish
Their absence is a metaphor
just like night is a ship
and the photo is an eelish moment

The woman folds sheets
under a gypsy sun
She can't count on living
stumbles into silence and fish bones

Her story is a
bruise on underwater skin
braiding rivers
the weariness of weather

Her past is a hesitation
a hovering voice
hands fading after endless repairs
to the dance of dust

Worry less about
the shouting wakeful moon
square-shouldered night

More about each ant bite of suspicion
the free-glide of traipsing tongues
all those birds in custody

If Words Were Fish

If words were fish
and fish were vessels

Boats would bob in the sea
round worried corks barnacled grey
woven centuries of sentence
harsh phrases hurtling the sides
hooks lines buckets nets
mashing words and wind

We fish for food and soul our spirit thin
look at our beaten faces say who are we stranger
The eyes of the mirror are shoals of fish
each is a vessel
a word

Each word
a container
Each eye a stab for dry ground

Soaked limbs drip over rough edge
splinter the smooth spread of red
where desert mouths meet tide

If words were fish
and fish were vessels

Never Turn Your Back

Never turn your back on the sea
he said the rocks cragging
at his salt skin the ocean rushing
his words into air his skill his knots
his swift knife
the fish tapping out its last breath
the scales the blunt gaping eye
Her falling cracking the deep blue
the indigo dark
The white wash as her body folds
Her sleek legs her reaching feet
her arms wrenched above
her crushing lids
her clenching saltpan mouth
her urgent lungs
His voice a rope net
brailing her dead weight
into the sodden boat
the wet the wood the rough
She opens her rock pool eyes
to a tarty sea anemone sun
Below her the water ancients
Before them the return inland
mutton-brown whip-crack dry

Memory

after *Vessels* by Anthony Whyte

White fish
Skilleting through water
It cups
Is a container for Blue Gold
Is clinker-built
Planked in bone
Fine as china

Is scripted flight
Wings describing voyage
A cobalt breast
One page of an open book
A single word
A vessel

Rainfall
Diminishing memory
Beyond recall

Difficult to Be Here

Georgia 2008

take over   rid   democracies   want   whole control
energy   routes   rid   regime   every democratic   rid
aggression   battle
ceasefire talks   long-term   hostilities
ceasefire   end troops   tanks bombs   retake
unnerved investors   sold   stocks
spiral   oil gas   rankled
widespread civilian   casualties   catastrophe
dead   homeless   bombing   civilian targets
anguish   innocent   clutching   difficult   to   be here

What Angel

What angel
is on guard over the woman
hoeing mud with raw fingers
or improvised blue plastic glove

What angel
fastens a floral wisp of headscarf
over her nose and mouth
against mass reek

cultivates the roses she would lay
on marked stone if she only had bones
for an apposite burial

helps the woman identify
the nap of home-sewn clothing
buttons stitched by her own hand

What angel
salves her keening gut
against human remains strewn
through a thick stew grave

What angel
was off-guard
instead of on watch
over so many sons

Red to Black

after *She Walks from Dark to Dark* by Kirsten Fairall

Red patent steps
night to night
Wet lawn shuffle
day to day
Shifting
Red to black
      Red to black

The green of her throat
her voice
Purple flight
Fingers leave grapes

Taxi

Suitcase flung into the boot the driver motions get in himself already one foot in the stirrup a horse race on the radio Has he a few dollars on? Oh mate he has to go home to his wife with no wage packet unless the last of his money is on the next start the commentator talking the horses into position a voice of jockey silk The gates open the crowd on its feet the thundering hooves the silk bright billowing the taxi filling with prayer I wish him luck I am to take him on a new course

His pick comes in and I am thanked over and over God bless the Irish he has lost two houses they are all on the edge but now there is $200 the winner accepts his prize the formalities and my case is handled with care his laminated skin the helpline posters in the hotels the TAB families gambling with the streets my belongings and I stand together on the kerb his praising eyes his unshaven skittish face leaking a smile I fear I may be embraced

www.ingramcontent.com/pod-product-compliance
Lightning Source LLC
Chambersburg PA
CBHW071509080526
44587CB00016B/2730